Published by Tigertail Productions
842 NW 9th Court
Miami, Florida 33136
www.tigertail.org

ISBN 0-9728808-3-6 [Volume IV]

Printed in the United States of America

Printed by Aquarius Press, Miami, Florida

Cover Photo:
Westen Charles

Design:
Vortex Communications

Project Coordinator:
David Beaty

Acknowledgments:
This book is made possible through generous support from Embraer.

Private support is provided by Al Alschuler, Shelly Baer, Tema Burk,
David Beaty, Andrea & Carlton Cole, Gail Foerster, Carolina Garcia-Aguilera,
Joan W. & Finlay Matheson, Gene C. Sulzberger, Thomas Swick & Hanna Matras
and Brenda Williamson.

Public support is provided by Audrey Love Charitable Foundation, Books & Books,
City of Coral Gables, City of Miami Beach Cultural Affairs Program, Cultural Arts
Council, Mellon Private Wealth Management, Miami-Dade County Department of
Cultural Affairs, the Miami-Dade Mayor and the Board of County Commissioners
and Vortex Communications.

VOLUME IV, 2006

Tigertail, A South Florida Poetry Annual

Edited and with an introduction by
Richard Blanco

Miami

Contents

Preface

In your hand is Volume IV of *Tigertail, A South Florida Poetry Annual*. I am writing this from a friend's home in São Paulo, Brazil, my place of the moment. In Richard Blanco's wonderful introduction he speaks about place and its complexities. This is the first issue of *Tigertail, A South Florida Poetry Annual* that includes poems by poets from outside of Florida, as well as a wonderful range of poets from this state. Next year we will publish a *Best Of* issue, edited by poet Max Winter; and the year after that a translation issue. *Tigertail, A South Florida Poetry Annual* is a living document that changes and responds to our community and the field. From my place in Brazil, as I write I hear the cries of the Vem-te-vi from nearby trees and the voices of street vendors below, each with a distinctive announcement of their wares. My adventure ends in a few days and yours is about to begin. Richard Blanco has made a wonderful selection of poems for this book.

Introduction

As a child of Cuban exiles, I could claim citizenship in three countries only forty-five days after my birth. Naturally, questions about home and place have figured significantly throughout my life and my poetry. But I've realized that these questions are actually very ancient and universal ones. The need to *dwell*—to exist in a given place or state—is a fundamental human desire, driving each of us to seek a unique physical as well as spiritual place in the world. Think about it: How much of life is spent engaged with questions of place and home, individually and collectively within our communities?

As allegory, the Judeo-Christian story of creation affords a powerful example of the fundamental connection between place and being. God first created a place—the Garden of Eden—which provided everything Adam and Eve needed in a state of perfect grace. Their eventual expulsion from their garden paradise suggests the nature of our perpetual desire to return to (or find) a place able to fully sustain and complete us once again; it also symbolically explains the void we feel and the hope we sustain in our wanderlust pursuits for such a proverbial Eden. Other examples of our quest for and connection to place surface in the form of myths throughout the psyche of human history, arts, and culture: from the ancient epics of Homer, to Atlantis, Avalon, and Aztlán, to the modern *Shangri-La*, *The Wizard of Oz*, and Peter Pan's *Neverland*.

But what *exactly* is place? What does it mean to say, *I'm a New Yorker*, or, *I'm a Southerner*? How do we come to call some place, a home? What makes Miami, *Miami*; or New Orleans, *New Orleans*; or Santa Fe, *Santa Fe*? Is it the architecture; the people; the climate; its history; our memories; or our imagination? These are some of the critical questions the poets in this volume ask as they explore the *Poetics of Place*, seeking to understand those measurable, as well as immeasurable, qualities of places, and our *place* in these *places*.

More than mere travelogues or memoirs, these works examine the complex ways in which memory, landscape, and imagination collide and intersect to form a sense of place.

Introduction *continued*

They represent place as a physical realm of tactile images and details, while also acknowledging that it is in some respects a human construct, a myth, an unreachable ideal that is ultimately indeterminable, and thus the subject of art. These poems recognize that we are three-dimensional beings who constantly live in the context of place; everything we experience and feel is located in some particular environment lodged in our psyche. These poets understand that where we live defines who we are in a very significant way; and, conversely, that who we are determines how we perceive our surroundings and where we choose to live. They address what is perhaps one of the most engaging and fundamental questions of human existence: *If you could live anywhere in the world, where would you live and why?*

As I finish this introduction I am sitting by a window overlooking the rocky coast of Maine in winter. In my mind I trace the coastline all the way south to my home in Miami Beach, and think of the birth of the Tigertail Poetry Annual, which originated as an anthology of South Florida writers. I am grateful to Mary Luft, David Beaty, and Tigertail Productions who whole-heartedly supported my vision to expand the themes of place in this year's volume by including forty-three poets from all over the country and other parts of the world. As I watch the waves crash futilely over the rocks jutting into the sea, I remember all the wonderful places I've been able to visit through these poets' words, as well as all the places I have lived or traveled through in pursuit of my own Eden. And, as snow falls over the beach, so far away from the warm shores of my Miami Beach, I recall what is most important in our contemplation of place: not what we can learn about it, but what each place teaches us about ourselves, who we are, and what it means to be alive—wherever we may be.

The Space Coast
Florida

An Airedale rolling through green frost,
cabbage palms pointing their accusing leaves
at whom, petulant waves breaking at my feet.
I ran from them. Nights, yellow lights
scoured sand. What was ever found
but women in skirts folded around the men
they loved that Friday? No one found me.
And how could that have been, here, where
even botanical names were recorded
and small roads mapped in red?
Night, the sky is black paper pecked with pinholes.
Tortoises push eggs into warm sand.
Was it too late to have come here?
Everything's discovered. Everything's spoken for.
The air smells of salt. My lover's body.
Perhaps it is too late. I want to run

the beach's length, because it never ends.
The barren beach. Airedales grow
fins on their hard heads, drowned surfers
resurface, and those little girls
who would not be called back to safety are found.

Published in *The American Literary Review*, Fall 2000

Cartography
after Neruda

I have no country.
My body is my map.
Myriad tributaries
flow in my limbs,
weave through twig
baskets of bones,
carry oceans of blood.

My nails are tiny barrier
islands, my hair seagrass,
eyes tidepools brimming
with sea creatures.
Shy snails inhabit
the shells of my ears.
Deer tread on the stones
of my wrists, the rocks
of my ankles.

When I breathe,
a gale fills my lungs,
a mistral, seasonal
siroccos. Rain water
collects in valleys—
on the inside of elbows,
the back of a knee,
the hollow in my neck,
in ridges alongside ribs.
It spreads over banks,
floods into caves,
drips into rainforests,
wet fingers reaching
for the dusty edges
of deserts.

I have no country,
no familiar soil,
no sacred ground
in which to lay my bones,
no grandparents buried
in the country of their birth.
My parents will not lie
in theirs, nor I in mine.

My body is my map,
skin topography,
borders bending
with the fate
of the disinherited
who bear their resources
to wherever wars,
dictators, or circumstance
fling them on the globe.

On a clear day,
I can trace
where I was born:
on an island shaped
like a sweet tobacco
leaf, hand-rolled,
lit with a flame,
deeply inhaled,
savored, smuggled
out, set free
to toss and travel
on a western sea.

My body is my map.
Everywhere I journey,
my land journeys with me.

The Album

for Orlando Rossardi

For a long time I've been besieged by carnal questions
like the why of a translucent bird's unheard song
or the rigidity of the vivid yellows
and greens in the rusty jungle of that photo
I took at the Parthenon and am now looking at.
And I ask myself about the footsteps that kneaded
the sand of the narrowest alley
that rises from Plaka straight to the Acropolis…
and about the smell of the Propylaea in its epoch of glory
and the sage words that covered the hill.

For a long time, when by chance I see them, I've asked myself
if those gray-haired ladies had been blondes or brunettes,
if their bodies had been a statue of Aphrodite.
And about their first love, O Zeus, and how many loved them
and about the horses and fish that let out their lofty moans
in pleasure for a near-eternal delirium.

For a long time I have questioned myself,
falling back into the confused beauty of my ruins,
and I notice that I have stopped asking myself about the future
and the nymphs that never were and the life that I invented,
and about the juvenile melody of the body and of the Hours,
the tender smile in the photos of fire and nard,
and I suffer at the cusp of my dead ciphers,
the subtle moment in which the *inquietudes**,
like the winds, changed forever.

Athens, March 17, 1998

* *Fighting causes, restlessness, concerns, ambitions.*

Translated by Yvette Neisser
From *El Testigo Se Desnuda,* Colección de Poesía Puerta de Alcalá,
Asociación Prometeo de Poesía, Madrid, Spain, 2002.

Barro

My name is *barro*, red sun
melted on the lap of love.
Caguana,
squatting over hot stones
to yield to my birth of sky.
I fling my hot breath to the world,
blessing and storm,
feeding my *maíz* soul
along the banks of my people's song.
I am the river
and the women who wash in it
but this is just to say
I am also the wind and *huracán*,
scent of blood in the fields,
worms beneath rocks.
I was born a slow dance
of cane and bamboo,

knocking always knocking.
Fertile or not,
I prepare for war now.
The earth is a woman who knows
bow and arrow.

West 16th Street

Light glossing on the breakers, then disappearing.
You say it is mortal that way: silver, then gone.
On the phone, it becomes the distance I listen for,
the waves talking just behind you. Here, it is quietly
confusing to be at this height, the city's colors

rising to an electric sky, its dense gray yellowed,
drawing from neons, chimneys, and windows
which declare themselves awake, for now.
For clarity, I pick one car pulsing among the red
sequence on the bridge; I follow to where its road

ends, headlights staring into a wall of trees.
You tell me how you were in the ocean for hours,
the heaving that took you under for deep seconds,
the salt warmth flowing from your nose and ears
long after you left the water. Tonight, you are

as far away as the house suddenly lit behind
the trees, a pond taking in the light rain, the leaves
dropping into it. The traffic on the bridge lessens,
some windows go out for the night. Sleep
might be a water shuddered into, or a mere falling.

It is not lasting mercy. It is only brightness or
it is dark. I cannot stop the surf from taking you in,
or the leaves from dissolving to silt. You stand
by the shoreline on another coast, and to me this
may be the form of perfect wanting, the logic

of a heart unsatisfied. But it is not purpose, it is
not proof. The meadow in the dream is polite
at first. Then wind slams every window and door,
testing the soundness of an argument. I will wake.
Something will be finished, the morning will be sad.

Published in *Pleiades*, 2003

Assateague Island

The Bay breathes all day, all night,
sighs against the sand, whispering small things—
of Sitka deer and willets, terrapins and gulls.
The sun hangs long,
then sets behind the salted marsh.

Dune grass blows.
Black-eyed Susans grow beside the swamp.
Crabs and salamanders hide among the weeds
while blue heron mince on stilts and freeze,
infinitely patient for a meal to spear and swallow.

Across the slender land,
the surf deserts itself like a lover,
rushes in tides and eddies towards the shore.
Like spiders, fishermen cast their silver lines.
Sandpipers, on unicycles, flirt with foam.

Pelicans dive pell-mell into the brine.
Water churns beneath a mackerel sky.
Barefoot along the slit eye of the strand,
we pocket the perfect moment to take home,
like a shell or smooth-shaped stone.

Shadow of the Family

No matter how large the house,
how green its walls,
how various its blossoms
or how small, brown
and gardenless—
at night each is a point
on the terrain: a brief remark
lit up and obscured,
different from the address
its family claims on documents,
different from the scent of its halls,
the isolating histories of its air.

Drive anywhere—
through the tropics, say,
in central Costa Rica
on unpaved roads,
past hills on fire on purpose,
past schools that are pavilions

awash by daybreak
with blue and white uniforms,
past rivers and lagoons,
the tag-ends of uncultivated palms
where even toucans are colorless
in the equatorial dark:

Drive out or drive back,
toward or away from some hope,
some place with chances,
and you'll think about
all the homes of all the people
you will never meet,
their positions on the land,
their proximity to or distance from
the road, their very stasis
relative as your own movement
(race of a shadow below a big moon)
yet what conviction it offers.

And you are hard to see
as all their roofs and porches,
your passage reducible
to headlights moving north,
however complete you may imagine yourself—
you *have* imagined yourself
walking a lamp-lit street
with your love,
the baby on your shoulders,
boy on his,
all four fixed within
a single silhouette:

a kingdom whose partitioning
anyone can chart.

Published in *Indiana Review* (Spring 1993—Vol. 16, No. 1) as
Sombra de la Familia and in the online journal *Beltway*.

First Winter in the New Neighborhood

I will go walking today. The cold is nothing next to
this longing for the city, for sidewalks and the salt
of how the winter is decorated. I would have it all—
dry skin, decaf, the Black people who glare at me
for moving into their neighborhood, the others
who smile. *You are not that interesting*, my friend
reminds me and I am freed, taught my own
irrelevance and sent invisible into the morning,
into observation.

Up here in the neighborhoods
grandmas die, babies fret all night, teenagers discover
pleasure and shame, women write songs, men cry,
children whine for this year's toy hawked
mercilessly on every TV in the city. We live.
The city holds us all, we are what she is
and in the morning, in a cold so surprising
for Washington, we turn to one another, we step outside.

Itutu Sankófa 2003

in memory of Ramón "Mongo" Santamaría

There will be people
        they said back in January
        that will leave us depart
while looking back at their people
—they said travelers from afar
we will see each other again—

One crisped a melodic conga solo
even while casket being lowered
after 83 years of
flying forward Sankófa-like
(bird who flies while looking at history)

Beginning when "Afro Blue"
inspired from a chant praising Obatálá
deep in the din of echoes
in Jesus María, La Habana
sounds that permeated cloth walls of el barrio's history
of central de azúcar, café, tabaco
like the scent of sopa de quimbombó

bollitos de caritas
proclaiming their scent through baroque streets
You flying forward while looking at history

In the time of "Watermelon Man"
you leaped through lines yr new country
was not willing to cross
You with golden rope of Santa Bárbara hanging
from yr neck entwined
in glass beads & sweat
thunder rolling from caramelo hands
celebrating how man is man—
"la clave no tiene color mi hermano"
said yr drum stained hands, Mongo
when they lowered la caja
yr last dance to a young rumbero's llanto
the goat-skins' lament praising
how you looked back into history
flying forward

A faint solo begins to play now
deep in el otro mundo
only you
can now chorus a response
kind of music you hear on tufts of clouds
yr quiet chorus now echoes here
where many mimic yr rhythm

Lying by your casket
was a red feather from an African Grey parrot
      (symbol of messengers)
though we're not in Cuba anymore
we're not in Africa anymore
still a red feather to chorus yr response

You keep flying forward
Sankófa-like
looking back into history at us
      your people

Note on text:
Itutu: In Afro-Cuban/Yoruba religion, burial rites for initiates; a sacrifice to cool,
and/or right a wrong.
Quimbombó: Okra
Bollitos de caritas: Fritters made from black-eyed peas.

Letter from West Virginia

If you ask what brings us here,
staring out of our lives

like animals in high grass,
I'd say it was what we had in common

with the other—the hum of a song we
believe in which can't be heard,

the sound of our own
luminous bodies rising just behind that hill,

the dream of a light which won't go out,
and a story we're never finished with.

We talk of things we cannot comprehend
so that you'll know about

the inner and the outer world which are the same.
Someone has to be with us in this,

and if you are, then,
you know us best. And I mean all of us,

the deer who leaves marks behind
in the snow, the red fox moving through the woods.

The same steam in them is in us too
although we are the chosen ones who speak.

Please tell me what you think cannot be sold
and I will say that's all there is:

the pain in our lives,
…the love we have…

We bring you these small seeds.
Do what you can with them.

What is found in the beleaguered
and beautiful land is what we write of.

From *Poems: New & Selected* (1993, reprinted 1994, Vision Library Publications)

I Like When You Are Gone

I like when you are gone,
our goodbyes said,
each returned to the separate homes.
To my good spouse—writing—
patient, pure, waiting for his meal.

I like the infinity of looking
at you from my housewife's life
without the infinity of you looking at me.
In short, I like to make you muse
when it amuses me.
What else am I to name you,
not my lover, husband, father, friend.

I like you from the opposite
bank of my imagination,
that shore I am no part of,
filled with its own weather and migrations,
bits of grass and feathers, flutter of griefs
I do not have to tender.

The moon, *corazón*, is the same
moon watching you, watching me,
the rain the same rain falling.

I like you at a distance waving
from twin banks. Hello, my new-
found acquaintance, my grain of sand.

You Should Have Seen It
(Connemara, Ireland)

What would it have been like before the train
Came west from Galway out to Clifden Bay?
What the trudge along the country lane,
What the turf smoke on the summer rain
When the Connemara coast was far away?

What music in the air beside these seas:
The lone bird over the marsh, the night
Horses feeding along the shore, the bees
Busy while the sun still warmed the breeze,
The lick of the ebbing tide before the light

Crept across the silver land and shone
Against the window through an interlace
Of mist and cloud, of heather, bog and bone;
And what love in placing stone on stone on stone
Against the wind in this forsaken place.

Today it is not remote, a bit out of the way
Perhaps: a few hours' drive and the roads are good
And still the grasses and the sea-thrift sway
Bending to the breeze above the bay
By the ruined castle. You should have seen it. You should…

But what would it have been like before the train
Came from Galway out to Clifden Bay?
What the walk along the country lane,
What the turf smoke on the summer rain
When the Connemara coast was far away?

Afternoon Screening of *Voyage to Italy* (1953)

I fell asleep and woke up in Tuscany,
the sound of a roadster
sailing through an alley of trees.

Who would not want to be European?

Always a street fair,
fresh figs and honeydew,
baskets of dry noodles and coffee beans,
bottles, passed around
between distant cousins,
paid for in coins.

The sadness of American women
exposed at last—

It takes an olive tree.
A bicycle leaning against a church.
A long stone path
upon which to hold her hand
and stroll to the aqueduct.

Did anyone even direct this?

Or did Enrico,
sad and drunk again,
leave his camera unattended,
cranked by the wind,
and here it is, a love story.

Beach Bunnies

Venus Clams (Veneridae) are probably the most successful of all the clams. Over 400 abundant species occur the world over. A flexible external ligament and a powerful muscle attached to the interior of the shells enable the animal to open its valves and close them to protect its soft body.

— from *Seashells in My Pocket*

1. *King Venus* (Southern Florida to the West Indies)

She's a wet-sand wallower, a sucker
for surfers named *Tulip* and *Sweet Limpid*,
her boogie board, slick with sea foam that hints
of underwater sex. Even the straight
mollusks rip off their goggles to watch her bait
deep-sea hooks, snag starfish, throw them back in
and head for MacDonald's. King's father's grin
was hers, even before her first bright tooth
bloomed above water. At night she's aloof,
pensive, a bruise in the sand, a figment
of her own detachment. King's spotted pigment
is hardly the envy of most Venuses
who prefer seaweed soup and real penises.
Silly clams. Only the Queen gets to fuck her.

2. *Elegant Venus* (Texas to the Caribbean)

This princess prefers silly clams around her
to out-of-reach-deep-sea types who dress
in green-thread algae. Elegant spends less
on clothes than…no one, come to think of it,
not even the glamorous *Textile Cone*, twit-
of-the-sea, not even tiny *Pertusa*.
Elegant is luscious wet. To lose her
would bring Mister Venus to the foamy edge
of her bristly purple shell. Uncaged,
she gulps down enough ocean for a bath,
enough sand for pearly intestines. Paths
all lead to Elegant, her soft body
a percussion of undertow, muddy,
delirious as the sea's fickle weather.

3. *Lightning Venus* (North Carolina to Brazil)

Crazy about delirious weather,
Lightning creates a good storm. Thunder booms,
typically, and she precedes it—zoom,
zap, cutting close to her lover's bones.
She aches, pulled palp and muscles, electric moans
that curl dulse leaves and tough eel grass.
Once she smoked an entire avalanche
of sea potatoes. It's her specialty:
beach peas, wrinkled rose, and link confetti
flash fried, a potion that works every time,
deadly as ink blood of octopi. Briny
ghosts follow Lightning's phosphorescent foot,
her shadowy imprint, her haloed hood—
the flash of her push, the flash of her lure.

4. *Golden Venus* (Philippines and East Asia)

One flashy mama, a pushy crone clam,
reef-famous Golden holds her own among
whipper-snappers, rappers and slackers, young
upstarts. Golden loves the sea when it's gray,
rusty treasure off the coast of Asia,
tilted ships pining on the ocean floor.
She's seen entire shorelines shift, sea wars,
and giant tourists in green water-wings
floating to paradise. Golden careens
down Ocean Boulevard like a pelican
on rollerblades, hungry and determined.
She hates being called ma'am, "Loving Care
Silver" all she ever uses on her hair,
the color of neap tides, dazzling star-streaked sand.

5. *Lettered Venus* (Indo-Pacific)

Her dazzling studies claim stars control tongues
and tides—*not* man or moon. Shocked academics
speculate about her bold linguistic
powers, wonder if her words predate God-
babble: the Koran, Torah, St. James, odd
holy books that read like dark fairy tales.
One day she woke with the lyrics of whales
imprinted on her back—their brackish mumblings,
disgruntled or ecstatic etched rumbles.
Anywhere words have been swallowed by the sea
she carries history, her body a key
to salty laws and knowledge that swells
from carp livers and the aortas of eels,
from the swordfish's sword, the lungfish's lung.

6. *Pointed Venus* (southern Florida, Texas, Mexico)

Pointed's got that sword-to-the-lung attitude.
Addicted to bivalve adrenalin,
she power-lunches with crestfallen
Sanguin Clams, gives them no-nonsense peptalks
re: *clam* defense, *clam*ouflage, and walking
like a *clam*-man. Pointed is all mer-woman,
fin-sharp and liquid, a lover of luminous debate. Once she fought off a whole school
of pacifists, detonating peace symbols
in the Gulf of Mexico. Pointed
wants to go where no *Venus* has gone—join
the *Volutes* in West Africa, pilgrimage
up the Mississippi to the edge
of fresh water, lethal ponds, forbidden food.

7. *Glory-of-the-Seas Venus* (North Carolina to Texas)

She's the Mother of Ponds, slick forbidden
deep-water siren who sings you to death
with her dolphin-inspired crystal-meth
melodies. *Venuses* worship her fluent
fluid ideas about valve-control, the Ten
Glorious Suggestions, earning her a place
of saint-like stardom in offshore bass-
holy waters. Glory is not only
Diva of the Deep, Bivalve Supreme, Roaring
Pink-Mouthed Queen, and Patron Saint of *Pismos*,
but she also conjures cures for dismal
beaches. She purifies polluted oceans,
tweaking the little toes of humans
who wallow in the wet sand sucking up clams.

Exquisite Politics, Tia Chuca Press, 1997

Thanksgiving

This was the first Thanksgiving with my wife's family,
sitting at the stained pine table in the dining room.
The wood stove coughed during her mother's prayer:
Amen and the gravy boat bobbing over fresh linen.
Her father stared into the mashed potatoes
and saw a white battleship floating in the gravy.
Still staring at the mashed potatoes, he began a soliloquy
about the new Navy missiles fired across miles of ocean,
how they could jump into the smokestack of a battleship.
"Now in Korea," he said, "I was a gunner and the people there
ate *kimch'i*, and it really stinks." Mother complained that no one
was eating the creamed onions. "*Eat, Daddy*." The creamed onions
look like eyeballs, I thought, and then said, "I wish I had missiles
like that." Daddy laughed a 1950's horror movie mad scientist laugh,
and told me he didn't have a missile, but he had his own cannon.
"*Daddy, eat the candied yams*," Mother hissed, as if he were
a liquored CIA spy telling secrets about military hardware
to some Puerto Rican janitor he met in a bar. "I'm a toolmaker.
I made the cannon myself," he announced, and left the table.
"Daddy's family has been here in the Connecticut Valley since 1680,"

Mother said. "There were Indians here once, but they left."
When I started dating her daughter, Mother called me a half-Black,
but now she spooned candied yams on my plate. I nibbled
at the candied yams. I remembered my own Thanksgivings
in the Bronx, turkey with *arroz y habichuelas* and *plátanos*,
and countless cousins swaying to *bugalú* on the record player
or roaring at my grandmother's Spanish punchlines in the kitchen,
the glowing of her cigarette like a firefly lost in the city. For years
I thought everyone ate rice and beans with turkey at Thanksgiving.
Daddy returned to the table with a cannon, steering the black
steel barrel. "Does that cannon go boom?" I asked. "I fire it
in the backyard at the tombstones," he said. "That cemetery bought
up all our farmland during the Depression. Now we only have
the house." He stared and said nothing, then glanced up suddenly,
like a ghost had tickled his ear. "Want to see me fire it?" he grinned.
"Daddy, fire the cannon after dessert," Mother said. "If I fire
the cannon, I have to take out the cannonballs first," he told me.
He tilted the cannon downward, and cannonballs dropped
from the barrel, thudding on the floor and rolling across
the brown braided rug. Grandmother praised the turkey's thighs,

said she would bring leftovers home to feed her Congo Gray parrot.
I walked with Daddy to the backyard, past the bullet holes
in the door and his pickup truck with the Confederate license plate.
He swiveled the cannon around to face the tombstones
on the other side of the backyard fence. "This way, if I hit anybody,
they're already dead," he declared. He stuffed half a charge
of gunpowder into the cannon, and lit the fuse. From the dining room,
Mother yelled, "*Daddy, no!*" Then the battlefield rumbled
under my feet. My head thundered. Smoke drifted over
the tombstones. Daddy laughed. And I thought: When the first
drunken Pilgrim dragged out the cannon at the first Thanksgiving—
that's when the Indians left.

Published in *A Mayan Astronomer in Hell's Kitchen*, W. W. Norton 2000

The Buick
1996

She buckles up her two little kids in the used sedan
and drives an American highway
away from last year's escape
across Cuban night waters,
away from her husband's death, her mother's.
Beastie Boys blare on the radio.
Her nail, lacquered "Mango-Dance" red,
punches another station: a commentary.
Afghan women wear heavy black *burqas*,
peer out from rectangles of thick netting.
Her windshield spatters with love-bugs,
the a/c chills her sleeveless arms.
Talibans wield metal-end sticks
that point to women's bare wrists.
They are "shameless" and chased over ditches.
The Buick speeds toward mountains with pines
as hushed as women who don't talk
about their hair or falling in love.
Ahead on Route 84 a school bus

carries laughing girls in blue jumpers.
An amputee waits beaten and jailed,
the reporter says, because she stepped through
a bus door reserved for men.
She shuts off the radio, the forest silent
like a woman's private pain.
Her children sleep,
and who but a woman in flight
would dream that a car the color of sky,
dripping oil and costing next to nothing
after burial debt, could wing her
wherever she wants.

Things That Bear Watching

(Nightfall, Rio Grande Gorge, 2004)

It goes chalky and grey, the color of lapsed coffee,
Then slate, charcoal, devil-dust inky, later,
And only the disposition of bridge shelves
Crisscrossing the hull scalped-out of the dark Rio
Below, daydream white, to guide the headlights of cars
Unused to night passing on 64 to Chama, and faraway West, *Beyond*,
Over the water—that, and the filmy sight of some loco coyote
Or marmot, the evening and Daystar, satellite winking in retrograde
Grooved to its elliptical black track, and always, *and always*,
The vagrant eyes of the poor come in from the fields
Shining across the splayed array of johnnystones, thistled shadowgrass,
Into the last things of this world that bear watching.

Published in *Southern Ocean Review: International Online Magazine of the Arts*,
Dunedin, New Zealand.

Corrida

...all stories if continued far enough end in death...
— Ernest Hemingway

It was for the novilladas, the beginners,
The matador, the flourishes,
And the backs turned on death
That I begged my father to take me to the bullfight
The summer we spent in Ciudad de Mexico
As far from the influences of drugs and sex
As he could remove me when I was seventeen
The last summer before I got pregnant.
He went with me everywhere: to the plaza
Bargaining for the silver trinkets for my sister and mother
To the bodega for the cigarettes
He let me smoke in front of him
To the pool where he sat upright, reading,
In hard shoes in the shade as I sunned myself, bored.
For the corrida we had sombra seats, the best,
Sparsely filled. As the sun's orange deepened
Town boys from the gradas came down,
Sat around us, sometimes reaching out
To touch my gringo hair. In the ring, I expected

The pirouettes with the muleta, color against dust.
Not the other red, cascading down the beast's black flanks—
To see the splattered velvets, matador, and hide,
To smell the pinkish foam, the bull's droplets mixed with sweat
When he shook his enormous neck,
The banderillas sinking deep, lodging in muscle,
fluttering vibrantly—I didn't expect.
One of the boys put an arm around me: *No mires, no mires*
He whispered into the air. My father stood
Scattering the boys like pigeons.
He smoothed the creases in his pants, appeared to stretch his legs,
Sat again, closer in the swelter,
Draped his arm across my shoulders.
The bull, front legs collapsed, shimmered,
Silenced, as my father and I were,
By the merciful, now, puntilla.
My father refused to let me accept an amputated ear,
Still warm, held up first to me, then to him,
The gesture for bravery, for not looking away.

Forgiveness

We could wade from that island into clear ocean
for hundreds of yards before the water
was even up to our knees.
We could sit there and watch small birds, and vultures
so high they hardly seemed to move.
We could walk out even further, to where the sand dropped off,
where the water was dark and muscular—
and we could push ourselves out into that dark deep
full of the ghosts of huge fish we feared
were fished out now, even while we shivered
with the fear of being watched from below.
We could swim out to a sand bar, almost out of sight.
We could stay out until dusk and swim back through the dark.
Or rain could start to fall, so hard we couldn't hear
each other, or ourselves. And sea birds—gulls and pelicans,
cormorants, terns, anhingas—could float
to that sand bar to wait out the rain. They could be
close enough to touch, all around us. And when the rain
stopped abruptly, they could take off

in a burst, all directions. The water could feel cold
as we swam back, and the surface we swam through
could be fresh enough to drink. And it could smell of flowers.

From *Flock And Shadow: New and Selected Poems* (New Rivers Press).

The Definition of Place
after A. Van Jordan

place (plās) n. [<Blk. org. jook-joint, *the spot*.] **1a)** bootleg house: there is a jukebox in the corner of this *place*, plays low down dirty blues, kind of blues that sings about a man holding on till help come along and if don't no help come along he still holding on. kind of blues where if the world stopped rotating on it's axis and fell into a corner pocket, everything be cool as long as he got a woman and a drink. **b)** building: this is a *place* where men in solid uniforms or Liberty overalls congregate for good times after wrestling with Mr. Charlie. **2a)** repose: as in *place* where iron ore strength can breathe easy, is a different nigger. the hornet's sting pacified by dollar shots straight down the throat, and the burn is heaven. a second home that is organic. can't be swayed by governor's office or state mandate that propagates: separate but never equal. this *place* got its own beauty. **b)** situation: women search this *place* for thickheavy fingers on breasts, live by darkness in shotgun houses on cement stilts with three kids and no daddy, wait for someone who can deliver them from foot tub washing. there are rooms with squeaky box springs; air filled with yesterday's loving and today's possibility. where ain't nobody mad but folks that ain't gettin' none. **3)** structure: space or *place* devoted esp. for specific purposes: to drink moonshine, play bid-whist, fuck, and have got-damn good time. **4)** region: a city/ a town/ a *place* called Birmingham where Negroes refuse to curl up and die.

New Hampshire, February 7, 2003

It's snowing again.
All day, reruns
of the blizzard of '78
newscasters vying
for bragging rights
how it was to go hungry
after they'd thumped
the vending machines empty
the weatherman clomping
four miles on snowshoes
to get to his mike
so he could explain
how three lows
could collide to create
a lineup of isobars
footage of state troopers
peering into the caked
windows of cars

backed up for white
miles on the interstate.

No reruns today
of the bombings in Vietnam
2 million civilians blown
apart, most of them children
under 16, children
always the least
able to dive
for cover when
all that tonnage bursts
from a blind sky.
Snow here is
weighting the pine trees
while we wait for the worst:
for war to begin.
Schools closed, how

the children
love a benign blizzard
a downhill scrimmage
of tubes and sleds. But who
remembers the blizzard
that burst on those other children?
Back then we called it
collateral damage
and will again.

From *Jack and Other New Poems*, W.W. Norton, 2005.

Tapas

White plates arrive in the shape of dreams
Deconstructed – a square of light, a nun's habit, a Grecian urn.
Barcelona's tentacles curl in a paste of red peppers.

Tonight the word "Spain" is neither geography nor history.
Tonight we say Spain like men say mermaid, *sirena* – we are
Sailors, as grateful in our course as we are unfortunate.

Tonight we say Spain like we say vinegar, earth,
Salt and sky – all things wearing away little by little
And accumulating.

Tonight virgin means saint
And the feet uncross themselves,
The body unbleeds itself from the wound

And we drink a wine of grapes, a wine of flowers,
We drink a wine of woodwinds and our throats
Open and close as the fingers press.

We say Galicia, Cataluña, el País Vasco, we praise
The rocks and ignore the sea that covers them.
Tonight, a tribe of three, we stare, pensive, across the fire

Recounting every formica counter, glass tabletop and iron skillet
Where we've discovered authentic and untouched
The Spanish omelette – doubloon-shaped tortillas we've tasted

In Lima, Vera Cruz, La Pequeña Habana, Cienfuegos.
It might be beautiful, says one. Or horrible, the other mulls –
This shipwreck, this salvation.

All Things Illegible

Divided by zero, the world upturns itself
as the Gulf opens its wounds to the sun.

The chill grows to a cold breeze
along the bubbles of foam fractaling

broken shell after broken shell,
each scattered piece a fraction

of what I need to know.
Silkened and fragile, the white sand

smudges its shadows—their work done,
like history—and kneads steeper ridges

where the sand greets the gates
of the houses facing the sea,

where seagrass leans against fence slats
as at the edge of the world the last

bleeding inch of sunlight streaks
across the water toward these shadows,

and even the approaching dark darkens
though when it arrives it has nothing to say.

Tulips in Miami?

All winter they burrow
in earthen folds
biding their time
before exploding
from wombs
that end up spent
and dormant
just so they may preen
on patches of land
no bigger than a box.

Some are cautious,
clenched and furious,
their refusal to open
a defense against
the heat. Others
are eager to show off
in spite of the weather
that insists

they do not belong
among swamp lilies
and saw plametto.

When you eye
the makeshift garden,
eager for a distraction
from the *Reguetón* revolution
blaring down the street,
you will overlook
the yellow creep of death,
how it spreads across leaves
that flounce like green boas.

Later, you will speak of
bouquets and second chances,
sip spring all day.

Memory of Pine, Blessing, *for Michael Hettich*

Piney Creek has no pines, only cottonwood line its banks.
Perhaps it remembers pines, in the fragrant way
memory conjures the scents of all that has passed away.
Tree memories are green and they scratch against
the surface of things the way dream branches
scar our trips to other landscapes where the constellations
glow strange and the rivers are much larger than creeks
and reflect back the mysteries of those alien stars.
But rivers of dream, like rivers in life, bear the sleeping
weight of all those cities and towns along the way,
the ones whose bridges link together fields and farms,
this neighborhood of Poles with that one of Puerto Ricans,
and best of all, those suspension bridges that cross
the waters in a miracle of flight. And the rivers of sleep
contain no mercury and the trout live happily
in those deeper places where no human
voice can pierce, and the water is pure enough
for all the dream animals to drink past midnight
and beyond in those silver hours before the dawn,

the one where creeks remember trees and human
sleep is filled with dream trout, and suspension
bridges fly off to beautiful meadows where one day
we will gather beyond this human life and sleep,
where one day we will learn the names of those
alien constellations, the ones that flicker forever,
the ones the creek remembers, the one it carries
like the memory of pine, yes, that memory of pine
which long-ago gave its blessing to this creek.

Sunday Phone Call

Dad cries in church: the First Presbyterian. It must be the music.
His Alzheimer's confusion growing, Mom calls, recounting obstacles.
I listen but hear only the flower and the unflower, the hard amazements
of grief and grace spoken by petal, pebble and feather.
And the darker cauldrons, how they bubble up in vapors and mists.

I get busy with spells; seeking a hook or frame to hang it all on:
a bone dance or incantation.
A solitary bird, I fly brazen with an old faith in breeze and buoyancy,
wheeling and scooting through indigo, a skydiver, rolling out like a gospel,
like Joseph of Arimathea or Mary Magdalene. Yes, she was there, too,
one more unlikely urban saint. For I do not attend the coat-of-many-colors church.

Instead, I fly westward Sundays over sawgrass at sunset,
towards the subtle feeding pools of the piano bird, known as anhinga,
towards the roseate spoonbill, the great blues, the ibis & snowy egret.

So Dad cries in church. It must be the music.
I'm singing now in languages that don't exist,
leaving behind histories and aspirations.
I'm so sorry; it must be the music.
Come along; Mom, Dad, I'm taking you with me.

We're winging it, westward, returned to mud and muck,
to that slow flow, a poultice, smooth as the refrains
of benediction, like leaves of—like a river of—grass.

Published in *Kinesis*, April 1997, Vol. 6 #4.

Tears

When I was growing up
icicles on Christmas trees
were called *lágrimas*, tears.

Decades later, in another country,
I passed the word on to my wife,
who grew up calling tears, icicles.

These days, when I get paid just
for musing, I wonder why icicles
melted into tears in Cuba.

There's more to this than water.
It's about the sadness of pine trees,
the grief of islands, the chill

of beatings and revolutions.
It's about my parents' marriage,
and illnesses and separations

and frailties too delicate to put
into words. It's about timing.
In my homeland, as in my home,

nothing could be less seasonable
than a Christmas without tears.

Is This Really Broad Street, Hartford?

Wherever I am the world comes after me.
— Mary Oliver

A stick leaning by the front wall
of the *bodega. Una caña.* A sugar cane.

What is she doing here surrounded by cigarette butts
and overripe tropical fruits which, by the look of them,
didn't survive the voyage?

All of us converging,
thousands of miles away from where we started,
our distorted reflections staring from small sections of glass
not yet covered with flyers for Café Bustelo
and laundry detergents on sale.

These fruits, this sugar cane, me.
What are we doing on this corner of Broad Street?
How long will it take before we start conjuring
tropical breezes and looking for the tormented
clouds of our islands?

San Luis Oriente, the small Cuban town
where I learned to say *caña,* to taste it, to want more.

Childhood games, pure, delicious like the sugar
cane we stole from the trains loaded at the Central Unión.
Boy heroes fighting to be the one to release the canes.

I want to grab the sugar cane on Broad Street,
dance with her. Run backwards.
Come, taste me, I hear her whispering. *Soy tan dulce.*

Yes. I must taste her again. *Esta caña tan dulce.*
I want to have her now as I did then. She wants
me to unveil her, to make her mine
in the middle of the street.

I close my lips around the meat
while she promises to take me
back, to be *tan dulce, tan dulce,*
like the afternoons in San Luis when the only thing
that mattered in our world was the sound of the train
enticing us *Sígueme, sígueme, sígueme, sígueme.*

Follow me, follow me, follow me. *Tengo caña*
tan dulce, tan dulce.

From *The Battlefield of Your Body*, Hill-Stead Museum Publications,
Farmington, CT, May, 2005.

Around Here

There are no literal translations:
a clay pan holds well water,

a woman stands in a closed
rice canal. Go back

to the beginning. See,
I'm still painting that river,

the Mississippi, not panoramic
but overlapping views

of the same place.
Around here,

you can paint all of the country
traditions that you want,

take a deep drink of air,
play phonograph records,

read books of poetry,
literature, the deepest

drink of my life,
but when I paint, I can feel

the curvature of this earth,
sense the size of this planet.

I am thinking now in French,
a new year of thirteen moons,

when you were a girl. Now,
who will take our picture?

Here are black and white
stones that can be raised,

lowered, altered like habits.
Here is a woman marking time,

here are thorns, and a child
who will die before her.

Published in *Dirty Swamp Poets*, September 2004.

Fond du Lac

At the heart of it, an ice rink, chinks
of waves stopped dead. A dressing mirror

for its own vanity. A pearl, stomped
flat by native gods before the French,

back when it was a glossy sheet
of blue, a basin filled with bass.

It might have become a ribbon
of water, slender and sexy,

overflowing west and south
to meet the Mississippi.

It might have been the biggest
of its kind: fresh water, inland, glacial;

might have grown to a great lake,
leading somewhere big like Michigan,

instead of staying here in town, pinning
the city to a map with a name immigrant

Germans couldn't say or understand:
Fond du Lac—*End of the lake, foot of the lak*e,

bottom? I grew up thinking *underwater*—
how the pressure of the place would

overtake us if we stayed around. Back
in my home town, where father's heart stopped

as he romped by the lake with his three
small children, I'm hoping for a trail marked

with three stones, or a map he carved in a birch.
But, no, just a surface mask of ice

undercut by current, a scalpel
from inside, its own flow lapping low.

Published in *Crab Orchard Review*, Volume 6, Number 2, Spring/Summer 2001 and *Family Business*, Finishing Line Press, May, 2005.

Digging Up Peonies

Overcoming fear of stalks that are too close,
I remind myself it's Lexington, that mist

on fields meant rattlesnakes in rows of corn
would be cold, sluggish. Like prying out

potatoes with my fingers, I dig up tubers
as if I could lift my father, seeded with cancer,

if only for a day from gravity, from ground.
My parents know what I know—this is the end.

They will not return to this house my father built.
No refugee in Kosovo, wheelbarrowing

his grandmother to safety, I will bring as much
of Kentucky, of their dirt as I can carry with me

on our flight to Connecticut. A bride, moving
to New Haven over thirty years ago, I have

not taken root. I cannot explain this urge
to go to creekstone fences my father stacked,

dig up box after box of peonies I will bank
into granite piled along my side garden.

My father will see pink, fuchsia, blossoming
from his bed. Is this what revision is, change

of location, spreading, to retell my story
another time, in another soil? Unable to untie

what binds me to Kentucky, to bones of all
those who are in my bones, I will save what

I can of my mother, of my father from this earth,
from the dissolution that binds us after all.

From *Gleanings: Old Poems, New Poems*,
Southeastern Louisiana University Press, 2003.

Morning Invocation, Taos
for Ebby Malmgren

Earlier than the first before first morning light
I've learned to wake, walking the chamber inside
the chamber that will unfold into waiting day.
See how the light comes across these walls, not
in fingers or poured honey, but as itself, particle
and wave, moment and time. I step outside, where
nothing can come between me and sky, between
the gravel caught in my boot and the cloud that
carries rain to the valley two valleys from mine.
Yes, to these mountains. Yes, to this life I leave
and pick up, leave and pick up. I ask the dawn,
not for blessing, but only to come, and come again,
in gusts of hummingbirds, handfuls of earth spread
on the air, circles of monarch wings, and a spilling yard
of sunflowers, balancing on thick stems the weight
of their heavy heads in the turning world.

From *Orpheus in the Park*, The Bunny and the Crocodile Press, 2005.

Evening in a New Town

When you're out walking you can allow yourself to be moved by the smell of roses, or to feel a twinge of pain at the sight of a lamp by a familiar-looking couch, or to feel as if you've entered a story when dusk falls and the streetlights across the bay twinkle through the fog, without realising how far you've descended or that if you go on much further you may never come back. But you always turn around at the right moment and return through the same streets, under lights dimmed by rich, dreary foliage. And, mounting the stairs, you find the same carpet and wallpaper and fixtures that you saw in a dozen windows along the way, and know that you've brought all the dust of the outer world into your own enclave. In a few minutes the rooms will have settled and become what they were to you, and yet for days afterward the window will let in a view that is hostile, with trees and houses that know your secrets.

Marsh View

From a window upstairs
you can watch the earth redesign
itself as mud, tall grass, and birds
as well as light, as well you must
stay drawn to shades of green,
ideals of green, all means of gold,
of russet, rust, colors beyond
association, barely earthbound.

You wake to the world the way
it ought to have remained, without
the squatters, the first of the big spenders.
Better to spend an hour at dawn
studying tides, deferring to songbirds
than measuring even your insignificance.
The window frames it all, the world contained
in its original skin, beyond your love.

Published in *Original Skin*, Peninsula College, Port Angeles, WA, 2004.

Snow at Dusk

Perhaps you are driving in the north country, the ache of long winters
numbed by stunted days—where each dusk counts in like a reckoning.
Daylight loiters as the sun deflates behind mountains, impassive.

Fallen snow inhales the sky's pale residue, brightness sighs out
across pastures, seeps under gates—bare trees, supplicants
to the fading light, reach up, fingers splayed, for more.

Civilization of fence posts, houses, out-buildings, the road itself
burned into this faint luster, an outline, an imposition,
a photographic negative that tries to reverse whatever is to come.

O love, O valor, a hero's emotions so diminutive at dusk, you think,
perhaps—life's ruckus a distant rumble from this car gliding
down a slick, dark road vanishing in the oncoming smoke of night.

Allegro *Con Salsa*

These Bennington College trees line the path
through the lake to my white-clapboard house
in Orchard C, godliness blue on the sifted, fresh
snow. This island boy can wither here, I think,
if not for the heat in my own blood, spooked
horses on my grandfather's farm, miles deep
in my memory. I cross the bridge, unsteady feet,
the snow crunches like bones under my boots.
The wind hits snow chunks off tree branches,
some nocturnal Morse code not intended for me,
but for some other creature. I start humming
an old song from childhood to steady my mind,
my tongue, my hands, my breath, frozen . . .
The moon peeks through clouds. I start to dance.
I conga through snow as if my life depended on it.

Detritus

What do rooms remember
what traces linger
on windowsill, ceiling fan, cupboard shelf?

Here a boy practiced violin
here another rolled a ball.
A mother cried quietly while they played.

Here a pan scarred the countertop
a refrigerator stamped the floor.
Here showers peeled paper, revealed more shells.

Shadows hang on empty walls
midday sun still fades the rug
gray, color of doves, of sky.

What's here can't be measured
but we can feel its breath
witness its steady, particulate dance.

Touch the chipped molding.
Trace a finger through plaster cracks.
Rest a hand on the sag in the stair.

Chiaroscuro: Night Market, Kumasi, Ghana

the night drinks the colors
      sucks them in
we are shadows
travelers get down from the truck
      eat in the night market
the merchandise is piled at the foot of
  some candles
      fried plantains
      fish
      kenke
I breathe
my shoulders droop
the cold sweat warms up
        I jump into darkness
    as if it's nothing
    the sunless blanket
    sucks our identity

now I'm not *bruni*
    white-skinned
      only shadows
  black-skinned
      only shadows
between your life and my life
    shadows
      nothing more.

Translation from the Spanish by Angela McEwan

Estuary

Adaptation is necessary here. Animals needing
mixture and movement. This is the annual resting
site, the pause in long days of flight, the vernal
and autumnal pit stop, a conjugal meeting of
salmon. Sand moves by saltation: small stones
skipping through the bed load, like POGs the
toy I used to collect from the bottom of juice
cartons, a game of discs slamming into discs,
pushing others away to get what you want.
We are searching for something to take home
and not kill. Dead sand dollars, white as teeth,
scatter on the surface. We frisbee them into
wind, white kites rising, displacing seagulls,
landing in a chuppah of cottonwoods. We
want the length of beach, smell of burning
driftwood. We want the meeting of two waters,
marriage of solutions, we want to be sluiced
by salt, we want our world as devoted as a
suttee, we want the diverse and sudden call
of death rising in wind, united in a shivaree
of waxwings holding an alter of air, the flash
of white shoulders, the final call for more.

Published in slightly different form in *Stringtown*, 2003.

camposantos

now
there is no one left to swaddle the acequias
if brown arms could reach out of this earth
they would

women in raven mantillas gather at noon
near the cusp of a chapel of heat-dried brick

above them the sun is a bowl
of mid-summer plums, blood-cerise turning
to purple, plucked from the sangre de cristos

amidst coyote fences and cast-iron railings,
locked cerquitas, wired once in old wicker,
each wife-mother caresses a marker wood

stakes born in stream bottom or splash-stone,
lip-reads words as *murió el dia* or *memoria*

kisses her crown of thorns, a rose, a heart
star, dove *pray for them madrecita maría*
we come to honor what has been
yet cannot be again

under day-star-of-noon, laden with wild lilies,
we plant our people's proud history land sky

farm   sisters of tecolote, mora, taos   we bless
these holy fields basking in the pueblos' thrall

among these gardens of the dead   luminescent
graves reflect lightning-on-silver slivers of God.

Published in *Manzanita Quarterly*, Winter, 2002.

2004

How was it I felt nothing
that last Ides of March
in the busy downtown square
of Largo Argentina
where Caesar felt the determined
point of conspirators?
All across Europe,
the morning papers read,
five minutes of silence
held for the Spanish dead:
that noon, the buses shifted
down and motorini slowed,
trailing fashionable scarves
flapping like standards on a field.
Why was it not quiet enough
for a personal public grief,
though Rome stood dutifully
observing more than itself?
The handsome Senegalese

stopped selling for the moment
their poetry against apartheid
while carabinieri hovered by
Pompey's portico latrine;
used exclusively by wild cats,
they spray the travertine. Goddess
of Fortune of the Present Day,
your temple is the rubble
venerated by Il Duce;
and the tired Communist Party
still prints the most colorful posters
competing with the Lotto sign
yellowing Berlusconi's eye.
A gypsy family that sleeps
three generations outside
split sandwiches, played cards
and waited to ask for change;
and the Bengal tiger stitched
on the father's leather back

stared down the promising awning
of the Chinese restaurant.
The warm sun reached us faithfully
through oceans of cool air,
the war had never ceased,
and all the art of the Renaissance
seemed part of this being fucked.
Then five minutes were up
and we heard the children shout
from across the ancient square
and release their bright balloons
into the afternoon air—
red and blue and gold
they rose above all things
ruined and not yet ruined,
perfected in themselves
disappearing from the world,
manmade yet natural shapes,
fresh as the painted birds

fading from Etruscan tombs
escaping the hunter's net
also depicted there
in the living necropolis.

Flamingo Sunset

While the bus horn bellowed, I knocked,
Swinging my swim bag, a dinghy maneuvering
Rough seas, received no answer.
Stepping into the room, I discovered a horror
Movie—*The Mom Who Turned Into a Dog*.
My hunched-over mother, her independent
Breasts as free-floating as limbs, clung
Drenched to my stepfather, beneath her
Opaque in the shadows, grunting.
Locked stiff, I backed out, clicking
The door tight behind me, never to knock again.

Age almost twelve, I boarded the bus bound
For day camp, advancing, with my body
Narrowed, breast buds filling their A cups,
Into Flamingos, the oldest girls. A blue-ribbon
Artist, I had spent weeks preparing pastel portraits
Of flamingos, plump and ruddy, their lush
Pink a stain on the memory, a cellophane
Wrapping masking the sky at dusk

While a flaming coral sun slunk from view.
At summer's end, that other stain
Would come, with its warm, dark stickiness.
"My little girl is a grown-up woman now,"
My mother would fuss, crying. What did I
Know then of stickiness—except for the grit
Of sand caked to Coppertone-coated
Skin, of ocean salt baked into sun-painted hair?
I knew of the damp, slowing confinement of Florida
Air, of geography's limits, my need
To speed things up, that would
In time transport me to a cold, fast
Place to finesse the art of bundling up,
Of layering. I was a girl still,
Curving and watchful but trusting the water,
Tucking up one leg, wading, all folded in.

Published in *The Antioch Review*, Fall 1993, and in
Conversations During Sleep, Anhinga Press, 1998.

Contributors

RICHARD BLANCO, *Editor*

Richard Blanco's acclaimed first book of poetry, *City of a Hundred Fires*, received the Agnes Starrett Poetry Prize from the University of Pittsburgh Press (1998). His second book, *Directions to The Beach of the Dead* (University of Arizona Press, 2005) further explores the universal themes of cultural identity, homecoming, and place. (www.Richard-Blanco.com)

WESTEN CHARLES, *Cover Artist*

Charles lives and works in Miami. He received a B.F.A. from Pratt Institute in New York and a M.F.A. from the University of Miami. In 1999, he co-founded Locust Projects, an important non-profit alternative venue in Miami. His work has been featured in exhibitions at Stephen Stux Gallery in New York, MOCA North Miami, Fort Lauderdale's Museum of Art and the Miami Art Museum, among others.

Poets of
Tigertail, A South Florida Poetry Annual

Note:

The following poets, Elisa Albo, Adrian Castro, Denise Duhamel, Zan Gay, Michael Hettich, Mia Leonin, Jesse Millner and Maureen Seaton have been published in previous issues of *Tigertail, A South Florida Poetry Annual*.

DEBORAH AGER

Deborah Ager's writing has appeared in *The Bloomsbury Review*, *The Georgia Review*, *Quarterly West*, and elsewhere. She's publisher and editor of *32 Poems Magazine*.

ELISA ALBO

Elisa Albo's chapbook *Passage to America* is forthcoming from March Street Press. She's teaching a new course at Broward Community College this year: "Food, Film and Literature."

LUIS ALBERTO AMBROGGIO

Luis Alberto Ambroggio is the author of nine collections of poetry published in Argentina, Costa Rica, Spain and the U.S. He was recently appointed to the North American Academy of the Spanish Language. In 2004 he won the Spanish TV Poetry Award.

NAOMI AYALA

Naomi Ayala is the author of *Wild Animals on the Moon* (Curbstone Press). Her poetry, translations, and reviews have appeared in several journals. A consultant, freelance writer, and teacher, she lives in Washington, D.C.

RICK BAROT

Rick Barot's first book of poems, *The Darker Fall*, was published by Sarabande Books in 2002. His second book, *Want*, will be published by Sarabande in 2007.

E. LOUISE BEACH

"A poet, librettist and translator, I count myself blessed to be working with words."

JODY BOLZ

Jody Bolz is the author of *A Lesson in Narrative Time* and an editor of *Poet Lore*. Her work has appeared in *Ploughshares* and many other literary journals.

SARAH BROWNING

Sarah Browning, an editor of *D.C. Poets Against the War*, has received an artist fellowship from the D.C. Arts Commission and the People Before Profits Poetry Prize.

ADRIAN CASTRO

Adrian Castro is a poet, performer, and interdisciplinary artist. He is the author of *Cantos to Blood & Honey* (Coffee House Press, 1997), and *Wise Fish* (Coffee House Press, 2005).

GRACE CAVALIERI

Grace Cavalieri is the author of fourteen books of poetry and twenty staged plays. She produces "The Poet and the Poem" on public radio.

SANDRA CISNEROS

Sandra Cisneros is the author of two collections of poetry; a children's book; a collection of short stories, *Woman Hollering Creek*; and two novels, *The House on Mango Street* and *Caramelo*.

STEPHEN CRIBARI

Stephen Cribari's poetry, plays and screenplays have been seen and heard for over forty years. He teaches law at the University of Minnesota.

P. SCOTT CUNNINGHAM

P. Scott Cunningham is an M.F.A. student at Florida International University, a Boca Raton native, and a proud member of the internet sites *My Space* and *Friendster*.

Poets

DENISE DUHAMEL
Denise Duhamel's most recent books are *Two and Two* (Pittsburgh, 2005) and *Mille et un Sentiments* (Firewheel, 2005). She teaches at Florida International University in Miami.

MARTÍN ESPADA
Martín Espada's seventh collection of poems is called *Alabanza: New and Selected Poems 1982-2002* (Norton). He teaches at the University of Massachusetts Amherst.

ZAN GAY
A native Floridian and Coral Springs resident, Zan Gay manages investment portfolios and land holdings. Her poetry has been published in *Tigertail, A South Florida Poetry Annual, Volume III*, *Enopoetica anthology*, *Runes*, *Rive Gauche*, *Feminist Studies*, and many others.

GTIMOTHY GORDON
GTimothy Gordon's recent books of poetry are *Everything Speaking Chinese*, Riverstone prize winner, and *Ground of This Blue Earth* (Mellen). His book-length manuscript, *From Falling*, was a Blue Light Press finalist; his poem, "Summer Rhythm," was a Pushcart nominee.

ELIZABETH HAUKAAS
Elizabeth Haukaas is currently an M.F.A. candidate at Warren Wilson College. Her work has appeared in various literary journals. She lives in New York City.

MICHAEL HETTICH
Michael Hettich's poetry has appeared in numerous journals and anthologies. Author of a number of books, he published two collections of poetry in 2005: *Swimmer Dreams* (Turning Point) and *Flock and Shadow: New and Selected Poems* (New Rivers Press).

RANDALL HORTON
Randall Horton is originally from Birmingham, Alabama. He is the current editor of *Warpland Journal* and his poetry has appeared in various journals and anthologies.

MAXINE KUMIN
Maxine Kumin's fifteenth collection, *Jack and Other New Poems*, was published in 2005. Among her awards are the Pulitzer Prize and the Harvard Arts Medal.

MIA LEONIN
Mia Leonin's book of poems, *Braid* was published by Anhinga Press. She is the 2005 recipient of an Individual Artist Fellowship from the State of Florida. She lives in Miami.

CHRISTOPHER LOUVET
A finalist for *The Bitter Oleander's* 2001 Frances Locke Memorial Poetry Award, Christopher Louvet currently lives in Miami.

CARIDAD MCCORMICK
Caridad McCormick writes from Miami. Her work has appeared in *The Sun* and *Generation Ñ*. She is also a columnist with *Now Playing Magazine*.

JESSE MILLNER
Jesse Millner is an instructor in the English department at Florida Gulf Coast University. He lives in Hollywood with his wife, Lyn, and dog, Sam.

SALLY NAYLOR
Living in Tennessee, Sally Naylor, a Miami exile, teacher and counselor, sends greetings to friends, former students, and fellow poets from the Florida International University M.F.A. program.

GUSTAVO PÉREZ FIRMAT

Gustavo Pérez Firmat teaches Spanish at Columbia University and is the author of several books of poetry, most recently *Scar Tissue* (Bilingual Press, 2005).

BESSY REYNA

Bessy Reyna is a poet, essayist, lecturer and an opinion columnist with the *Hartford Courant*. Her work has appeared in numerous anthologies in the U.S. and Latin America. (www.bessyreyna.com)

HOLLY A. SCHULLO

Holly Ann Schullo is completing a Ph.D. at University of Louisiana Lafayette, with recent work in *Louisiana Literature*, *Interdisciplinary Humanities*, *Poems and Plays*, *Literary Mama*, and *Yemassee*.

MAUREEN SEATON

Maureen Seaton's *Venus Examines Her Breast* (Carnegie Mellon, 2004) won the Publishing Triangle's Audre Lorde Award. She directs the Creative Writing program at the University of Miami.

PAULA SERGI

From August through October, 2005, Paula Sergi served as Wisconsin's cultural ambassador to sister state, Hessen, Germany, where she ate wienerschnitzel and wrote poems.

VIVIAN SHIPLEY

The Connecticut State University Distinguished Professor and Editor of *Connecticut Review*, Vivian Shipley won the 2005 Lifetime Achievement Award for Service to the Literary Community from the Library of Congress Connecticut Center for the Book.

ROSE SOLARI

Rose Solari has authored two full-length collections of poetry, *Orpheus in the Park* (2005) and *Difficult Weather* (1994). Her work has appeared in many journals and anthologies, including *American Poetry: The Next Generation* (Carnegie Mellon, 2000).

WANDA WATERMAN ST. LOUIS

Wanda Waterman St. Louis is a psychology student, a musician and a freelance writer. She lives in a log cabin in the woods in Nova Scotia.

DAVID STARNES

David Starnes teaches writing at Georgia Southern University, Statesboro. His chapbook, *Original Skin*, was published in 2004 by Peninsula College in Washington State.

JENEVA STONE

Jeneva Stone's poems have appeared in *New Hampshire Review*, with work forthcoming in *Colorado Review*. Her blog on poetry, motherhood, and politics is at www.jgirl3.blogspot.com.

VIRGIL SUÁREZ

Virgil Suárez was born in Havana, Cuba. His latest book of poetry is *90 Miles: Selected and New*, published by the University of Pittsburgh Press. He loves the city of Miami.

MARIANNE TAYLOR

Marianne Taylor lives in a small Iowa town with her husband and four sons. She received the 2004 Allen Ginsberg Award and has published widely.

LILIANA VALENZUELA

Liliana Valenzuela is a poet, writer, and literary translator. Her poetry chapbooks are *Bocas palabras*, *Mujer frontera*, *mujer Malinche*, and *The Poetry of Rice Fields*.

JEREMY VOIGT

Jeremy Voigt has worked as a dockhand, a janitor, a disc jockey, a saxophone instructor, a webmaster, a book slinger, and a substitute teacher.

Poets

ANDREA L. WATSON

Andrea L. Watson's show, *Braided Lives: A Collaboration Between Artists and Poets,* was sponsored by Taos Institute of Arts in 2003 and traveled to San Francisco's SomArts Cultural Center in 2005.

JOSHUA WEINER

Joshua Weiner is the author of *The World's Room* (Chicago). *From the Book of Giants* will be published in the fall of 2006 (Chicago). He lives in Washington D.C.

MICHELE WOLF

Michele Wolf's *Conversations During Sleep* won the Anhinga Prize for Poetry. Her poems have appeared in *Poetry*, *The Hudson Review*, *North American Review*, and elsewhere.